U.S.A.A.F AIRCRAFT WEAPONS OF W.W.II

Contents

ACKNOWLEDGEMENT

Hunting down the details of eighty-year-old weapons systems can be rather frustrating, but I get by with the help of my friends. Many thanks to Bruce Canfield, Marty Morgan, Rick Shab, Alex Antonopoulos and Jim Wagner for your kind assistance and expert guidance.

Tom Laemlein

U.S.A.A.F AIRCRAFT WEAPONS OF W.W. II

ISBN 978-91-984776-0-3
Design: Toni Canfora
Print: Finidr s.r.o, Czech Republic

Canfora Publishing / Grafisk Form&Förlag
Upplandsgatan 96A
113 44 Stockholm, Sweden
info@canfora.se
www.canfora.se

Introduction

BOYHOOD DREAMS

Looking at these photos, it reminds me that even old boys can still be young again, dreaming of piloting Mustangs or Thunderbolts, or manning the top turret of a B-17, hammering away with trusty .50 caliber Browning machine guns and knocking down Bf109s, Fw190s, Zeros, and Oscars like so many clay pigeons in a shooting gallery.

When I brought up the concept of this book to my publisher Toni Canfora, I found that he had the same kind of dreams while he was growing up in Sweden. As we worked on the design, we struggled to cut any photos from the layout, and instead added more images, and more pages than originally planned. It was a labor of love. As you look through these wartime images, I hope they bring back the excitement and adventure of your youthful imagination, and that they provide the inspiration for your next detailed model, or research project, or they simply enhance your appreciation of aviation history and the intense battle for the skies during World War II.

GREAT WAR BEGINNINGS

When America entered into World War One in April 1917, the country had a tiny military, and almost no military aviation organization. Machine guns were scarce, and automatic weapons that were appropriate for aerial combat even more so. Within a year, that situation had dramatically changed, and American industry was rapidly becoming the Arsenal of Democracy.

Before World War One, US Army Captain Charles Chandler became the first to fire a machine gun (a prototype Lewis gun) from an aircraft—a Wright Model B on June 7, 1912. The Lewis gun would go on to license manufactured in England, and also at Savage Arms Company in the USA. Many of these Lewis guns were built in an aircraft configuration, equipped with standard 47-round magazines, and the expanded 97-round aircraft variant.

US combat aircraft in WWI were supplied by the French and British, and consequently the British Vickers gun (chambered in .303) was provided as the forward-firing, synchronized gun armament. Lewis guns were used in the observer's position of US Army Air Service aircraft, many of them chambered in British .303, with some late war examples of the M1918 Lewis (in US .30 caliber) provided as well. Late in the war, a small amount of the Marlin Model 1917 (7 MG) were used as synchronized guns by the US Army Air Service. The Marlin gun was a redesign of the Colt-Browning M1895 (the "Potato Digger"), modernized to use a straight gas piston action instead of the original, unique

The machine gun takes flight: US Army Captain Charles Chandler, holding a .30 caliber Lewis gun, fired the first airborne machine gun on June 7, 1912.

Early US bombing efforts were rudimentary and quite personal.

US Army Air Service cadet fusing 20-pound bombs attached to simple racks. Stateside training, early 1918.

The observer's position: Twin (.303) Lewis guns on a Scarff mount aboard a French-built Bréguet 14 of the US 96th Aero Squadron. France 1918.

The forward-firing Vickers MG (.303) of a Bréguet 14 of the US 96th Aero Squadron. France 1918.

swinging arm. As the Marlin fired from a closed bolt it was suitable to synchronize to fire through the aircraft propeller. The Marlin MG was also eight pounds lighter than the Vickers MG (25 vs. 33 lbs).

THE BROWNING AIRCRAFT GUNS

John Moses Browning was a genius weapons designer and his machine gun creations would provide most of America's combat aircraft armament through the Korean War. Browning began working on a fast-firing, air-cooled .30 caliber machine during 1918. His initial design work proved fruitful and he developed the famous M1919 family of .30 caliber MGs. The initial US Army Air Corps machine gun was the Browning M2, which was standardized for aircraft use in February 1930. The M2 fired much faster than the similar weapons designed for ground use and was available as either a "fixed" or "flexible" gun. Fixed guns were rigidly mounted in the wings or forward fuselage, and flexible guns were mounted on a rotating mount for observers, or in a socket mount for bomber gunners. The gun was fed by a metal, disintegrating link belt. Armor-piercing and incendiary/tracer ammunition was created for aircraft use.

At the same time, John Browning sought to give America fire superiority in the air. Work on his massive .50 caliber heavy machine gun began even as WWI was ending. The initial Browning M1921 .50 caliber MGs did not perform particularly well during trials, and initial suspicions were that the big MGs were not suitable for aircraft use. Work continued and by 1939 the Browning M2 series had been created, and the M2 aircraft gun was able to fire 600 rounds per minute. During the next three years the M2's cyclic rate was increased to 850 rounds per minute.

The US Army and Navy rarely agree on anything, but they did find consensus on the Browning aircraft MGs. Consequently, the weapons were given a common nomenclature: The Browning .30 caliber AN/M2 machine gun, or the Browning .50 caliber AN/M2 machine gun. The "AN" stands for "Army-Navy" and the caliber denotes the weapon type. Both were available in "fixed" or "flexible" variations, with fixed guns fired by the pilot with an electrically operated re-

British guns, French fighter, American ace: The twin Vickers MGs (.303) of the SPAD S.XIII, the mount of Captain Eddie Rickenbacker, America's leading ace in WWI with 26 victories. Each Vickers MG was provided with 400 rounds, and the guns could be fired together or separately.

Salmson 2 A.2 recon aircraft of the US 91st Aero Squadron in 1918. The US purchased 700 of the French Salmson 2s, and they generally performed well. Armament consisted of one Vickers mounted above the engine and a pair of Lewis guns for the observer.

motely mounted solenoid trigger. Flexible guns were fired by a gunner using a butterfly trigger between spade grips. The weapons featured a light barrel that was easily cooled by the aircraft's slip stream.

ARMING USAAF FIGHTERS AND BOMBERS

The .30 caliber AN/M2 was an extremely fast-firing gun, cycling at up to 1,500 rounds per minute. The similar British Browning, the MKII (chambered in .303) cycled at about 1,200 rounds per minute. In the early war period, these weapons were sufficient for attacking enemy fighters and light bombers, but they struggled to bring down more strongly constructed bombers. Also, the .30 caliber MGs' range was critically short. After 1942, the .30 caliber AN/M2 disappeared from most USAAF combat aircraft.

The big .50 caliber AN/M2 quickly became the dominant aerial weapon in the American arsenal. The .50 caliber AN/M2's powerful 12.7x99mm cartridge was effective against enemy aircraft out to approximately 700 yards, smashing through wings, fuselages, fuel tanks, and cockpits. Even late-war Axis aircraft were rarely so well protected as to resist an accurate barrage of .50 caliber fire. The usual ammunition load for the .50 caliber AN/M2 included armor-piercing (AP), armor-piercing incendiary (API), and armor-piercing incendiary tracer (APIT) rounds.

The Boeing B-17 "Flying Fortress" was aptly named, and the fort's defenses rapidly increased from four .50 caliber guns and one .30 caliber MG in the B-17C, to a whopping thirteen .50 caliber AN/M2 Browning guns in the B-17G. A formation of B-17s, or B-24

American observers training with twin Lewis guns on a Scarff mount. This appears to be a US-made M1918 Lewis aircraft gun (manufactured by Savage), chambered in .30 caliber. With the 96 Aero Squadron, France 1918.

Comical looking, but the training was deadly serious. US Air Service cadet during stateside training in 1918. The trainer is equipped with a Marlin M1918 aircraft machine gun in .30 caliber. Ultimately, 22 US squadrons were equipped with Marlin MGs by the end of 1918.

Liberators, could bring several hundred .50 caliber guns to bear in almost any direction. German pilots began to attack from the front, where the bombers defensive fire was normally the weakest. Ultimately, additional armament was placed in the nose of B-17s and B-24s, but the head-on attacks remained the enemy's best bet when equipped with standard armament. The Germans tried rockets and cannons (37mm and 50mm) to attack the bomber formations from outside the range of the .50 caliber MGs – only finding occasional success. Even unescorted daylight raids were never turned back.

STRAFING AND GUNSHIPS

The .50 caliber MGs proved to be both powerful and accurate. USAAF fighters normally carried the .50 caliber weapons in their wings, and this required gun "harmonization" and creating a point of convergence, generally about 1,000 feet ahead of the fighter. When the .50 caliber MGs could be centralized and focused, as in the nose of the P-38 Lightning, accuracy and firepower improved. In the bitter struggles of the Solomon Islands campaign, USAAF units created potent strafing "gunships" by clustering up to eight .50 caliber guns in field-modified mounts within the noses of B-25 and A-20 bombers. Initially the additional Browning MGs and the ammunition had to be begged, borrowed, or stolen. As the gunship concept quickly proved its worth, the stateside production facilities began to turn out factory-built aircraft with a "strafer nose" mounting multiple forward-firing .50 caliber MGs. By 1944, the B-25J was equipped with twelve fixed .50 caliber guns in the nose, and

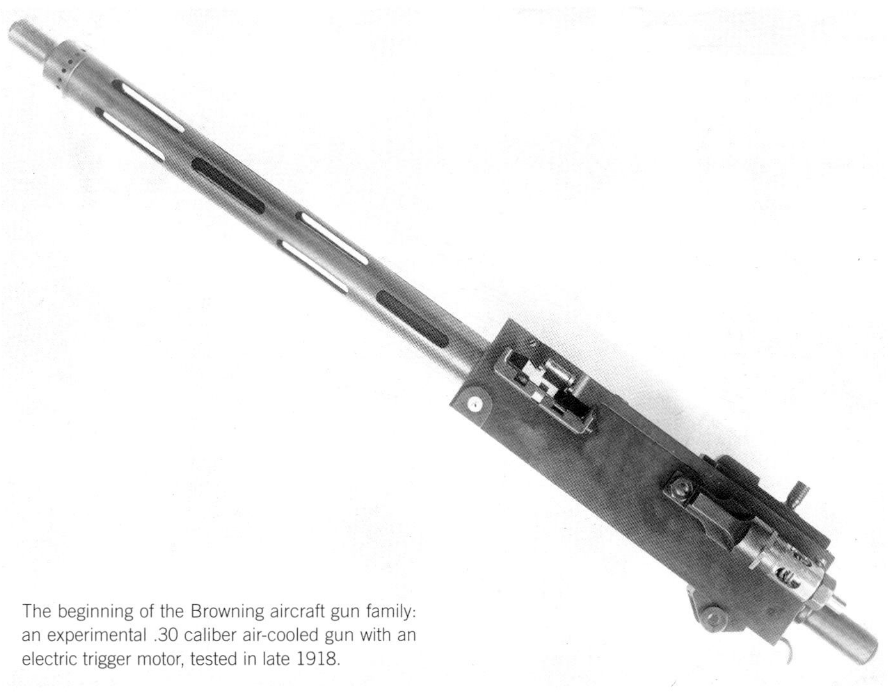

The beginning of the Browning aircraft gun family: an experimental .30 caliber air-cooled gun with an electric trigger motor, tested in late 1918.

The breech of the Browning AN/M2, which could be set up to feed from either the left or the right side.

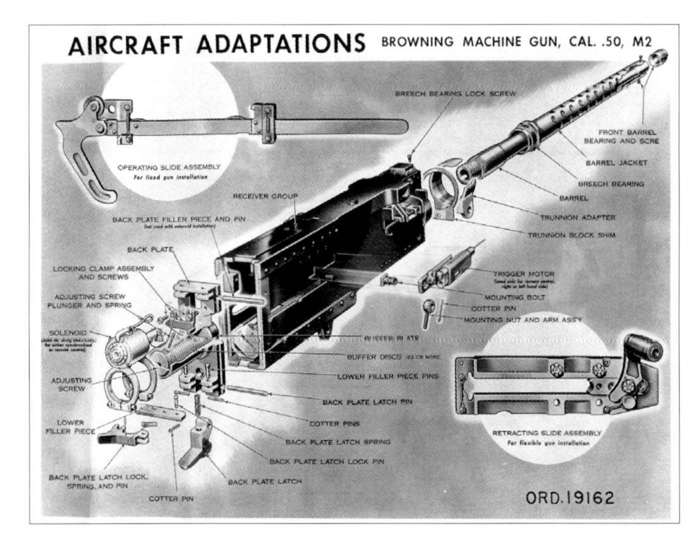

The gun that shot down the Axis: The Browning .50 caliber AN/M2 machine gun.

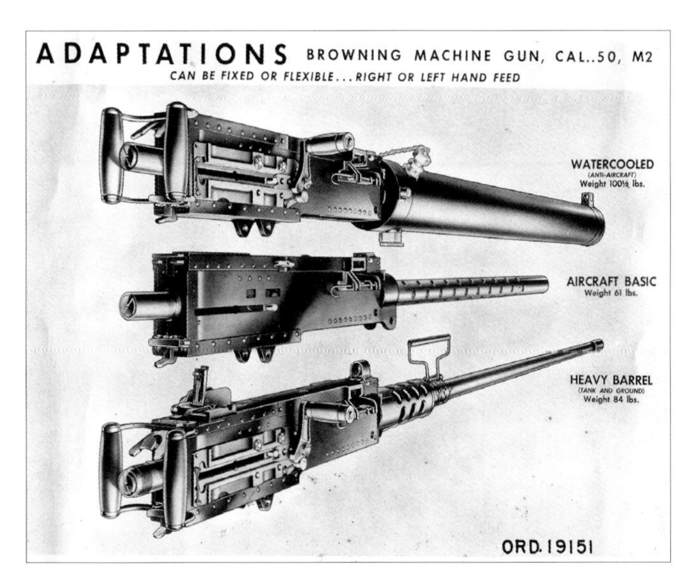

The Browning M2 variants: the water-cooled gun was used primarily in the anti-aircraft role, while the M2 heavy barrel was normally mounted on vehicles. The Browning M2 remains in service, essentially unchanged, to this day.

Bell YFM-1 Airacuda bomber interceptor, introduced in February 1940. Each nacelle was equipped with a 37mm T9 cannon and a co-axial Browning .30 caliber AN/M2 MG. Bell interceptors were ahead of their time, but handicapped by under-performing aircraft and unreliable cannon armament.

The Bell P-39 Airacobra with its nose-mounted 37mm M4 autocannon. Designed by Browning Arms and manufactured by Colt, the M4 was fed by a 30-round "endless belt" and cycled at 150 rounds per minute.

if the top turret gunner was willing, he could add his two for a total of fourteen .50 caliber MGs available for strafing. Small wonder that the Browning .50 caliber MGs are called the guns that shot down the Axis.

CANNONS MORE OR LESS

Like most other WWII air forces, the USAAF sought to develop more effective cannon armament. In this area the American arsenal found mixed results. The 20mm AN/M2 aircraft cannon was an American-built version of the British Hispano 20mm gun with a slightly longer chamber that proved prone to misfires from a lightly struck primer. The American M2 has been described as "unreliable" and also "unimpressive" and was rarely used as a wing-mounted gun. When used in the nose of the P-38 Lightning, the M2's performance was aided by the aircraft's built-in cocking system, allowing for an easy re-cock after a misfire. The P-61 Black Widow also used the M2 cannons effectively in a four-gun package mounted in the belly. In the overall however, the M2 20mm cannons never became the standard US fighter armament, and the .50 caliber AN/M2 machine guns remained standard until the early 1950s.

Even today, there is still much confusion about the 37mm M4 autocannon of the P-39 Airacobra and P-63 King Cobra. The P-39 was originally designed as a bomber interceptor, and its 37mm gun was always intended for use against aircraft. The M4 autocannon is a low velocity weapon (2,000 fps muzzle velocity), and slow firing as well (150 rpm). The 37mm rounds are relatively short ranged as well. It was never designed for use as a "tank-buster", and with its low velocity ammunition the M4 autocannon would be useless in that role. To be clear, neither the USAAF or the Soviets used the P-39 as a tank-buster – armor-piercing ammunition for the 37mm gun wasn't even supplied to the Red Air Force. However, in air-to-air combat the Soviets made good use of the M54 HE round with its shattering effect on enemy aircraft.

ROCKETS AND TANK-BUSTING

The powerful armament carried by most USAAF fighters led to an easy transition into the fighter-bomber role, and the .50 caliber guns were excellent weapons for strafing. Soft-skinned and lightly armored vehicles, including locomotives and warships up to destroyer-escort size were vulnerable to the concentrated fire of the Browning guns.

In the late spring of 1944, the 4.5-inch M8 rockets reported for duty with little fanfare and even less training. Fighter pilots had to learn on-the-job how to use the unguided rockets fired from the heavy and awkward M10 triple tubes. I spent some time interviewing several 9th Air Force P-47 pilots and few had anything good to say about the rockets, as the M8 was handicapped by short range, was inaccurate, and the triple tubes added plenty of drag, even for the powerful Thunderbolt. The tubes could be jettisoned but in doing so the pilot faced the wrath of his crew chief, as few replacement tubes were available. As 1944 wore on, many squadrons quietly retired the impressive looking "rocket guns" that rarely hit anything.

Loading the 40-pound, 4.5-inch M8 rocket into the M10 triple tube launcher mounted on a P-47 Thunderbolt. Despite the impressive appearance of the "rocket guns", the M8 rocket was inaccurate and the weapon system faded from use by early 1945.

Even though the Korean War saw many new aircraft in service with US Air Force, several WWII-veteran planes were still flying. The Mustang, redesignated "F-51" during 1947 continued to serve, although in the role of a ground attack aircraft.

Modern video games and flight simulators have re-energized the myths about the effectiveness of tactical airstrikes against German tanks. Wartime examinations of knocked out German AFVs showed that they were rarely destroyed specifically by air attacks, but that doesn't mean that the fighter-bombers weren't effective. The machine guns, rockets and bombs used in repeated strafing attacks devastated German troop formations and tore their supply lines to shreds. A Tiger or Panther tank needed plenty of support, and a tank abandoned due to the lack of fuel, spare parts, or the mechanics to repair it was just as dead as if hit by a bomb or rocket. Tank-busting was a much more compelling story to tell than the wholesale destruction of German road and rail transport.

INTO THE JET AGE

As World War II was ending, the USAAF finally got the Browning .50 caliber machine they had wanted since 1940: the fast firing AN/M3. The M3 cycled at up to 1,300 rounds per minute, and while less than 2,500 of M3s were built by the war's end, some found their way into the nose of the P-80 jet fighters that saw some combat testing in Europe in April 1945. Development continued after the war and with some smart redesign and use of advanced metallurgy the AN/M3 equipped the US Air Force's F-86 Sabre in its battles over MiG Alley during the Korean War.

Preparing for battle over MiG Alley in Korea: this North American F-86 Sabre shows off its weapons bay containing six fast-firing (1,300 rpm) .50 caliber Browning AN/M3 MGs with 300 rounds per gun.

MACHINE GUNS AND CANNONS AS OFFENSIVE WEAPONS

"Scrapiron IV" a P-38J Lightning of the 367th Fighter Group. The Lightning was armed with four Browning .50 caliber AN/M2 machine guns and one M2 20mm cannon, all mounted in the nose. Juvincourt, France September 1944.

The guns of the "Texas Ranger": P-38J flown by Lt. Colonel Jack Jenkins of the 38th Fighter Squadron, November 1943. Jenkins was the first pilot to score a kill flying the P-38 with the 8th Air Force.

Captain Owen Hanson, flight leader in the 392nd Fighter Squadron, comparing the 20mm and .50 caliber cartridges used in the guns of the P-38J. France, October 1944.

P-38J Arkansas Traveler of the 367th Fighter Group, Clastres, France, October 1944. The 20mm M2 cannon was found to be unreliable in other USAAF aircraft, but the P-38 had a built-in cocking system that allowed the gun to be re-cocked after a light strike from the firing pin failed to detonate the primer.

P-38 of the 94th Fighter Squadron on Corsica. Note the ejection chutes for the spent .50 caliber casings and the chrome thermal sleeves on the aircraft's machine gun barrels.

Flying scoreboard: The P-38's concentrated firepower was particularly effective on the more lightly constructed Japanese aircraft. More than 100 USAAF pilots became aces flying the P-38 in the Pacific theater, including the leading two.

P-38 ace's mount on Guadalcanal. The Lightning's centralized armament created more accurate shooting out to 1,000 yards.

The installation of all the guns on the P-38 made the weapons package particularly accurate—the shot pattern was the same at all ranges, and there was no need to estimate for "convergence".

"Shoot you're faded": The P-38's 20mm M2 cannon was a gas-operated, delayed blowback, belt-fed weapon (150 round belt). The M2 cycled at 750 rounds per minute, and its 20mm rounds travelled at 2,800 feet per second.

P-38J Bambi of the 338th Fighter Squadron, England, May 1944. Note the thermal sleeves on the Lightning's gun barrels.

P-38 on the deck: strafing practice in the Panama Canal Zone. The Lightning's centrally concentrated provided greater range and accuracy than USAAF fighters with wing-mounted guns.

P-38 gun camera film in the PTO. 20mm M2 cannon is in the center, surrounded by the .50 caliber Browning MGs. The AN-N6 16mm gun sight aim point (GSAP) camera was made by Fairchild Camera & Instrument, with the film magazine made by Eastman Kodak.

The P-39Q-1 was armed with the standard M4 37mm autocannon and replaced the wing-mounted .30 caliber MGs with underwing .50 caliber MG pods, with 300 rounds of ammunition each. Bougainville, December 1943.

The nose-mounted .50 caliber Browning MGs (200 rounds per gun) of the Bell P-39D-1 Airacobra. This aircraft is seen in Iceland during February 1942.

Due to shortages of the 37mm M4 cannon, the P-39D-1 used the M1 20mm cannon. The M1 used a 60-round drum magazine and cycled at 600 to 700 rounds per minute. Seen with the 40th Fighter Squadron in New Guinea during early 1943.

P-39D-BE during 1942. The Airacobra's 37mm M4, with hydraulically controlled recoil, was designed by Browning and built by Colt. Its M6 "Horsecollar" endless belt magazine held 30 rounds of 37x145mm High Explosive-Tracer (HE-T) ammo. The M4 cycles at 150 rounds per minute and its 37mm ammo travels at 2,000 feet per second.

P-39D-1 equipped with 20mm M1 cannon. Even though the M1 had problems of its own, many pilots found the 20mm gun to jam far less than the P-39's normal 37mm M4 cannon. With the 39th Fighter Squadron, Australia, late 1942.

"Spare Parts" was P-39 rebuilt as a night-fighter in the Southwest Pacific in March 1944. The .30 caliber wing MGs have been deleted but the M4 37mm autocannon and the two .50 caliber Browning MGs in the nose have been retained.

The P-400 was an export version of the Bell P-39, equipped with the 20mm M1 gun (a copy of the British Hispano) instead of the normal 37mm autocannon. This shark-mouth example is seen on Henderson Field, Guadalcanal during the late summer of 1942.

The Bell P-400 in England. The P-400 was not liked by the British, and ultimately flew just one combat mission in RAF service.

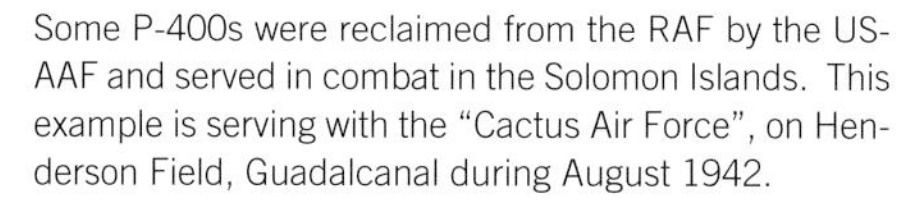

Some P-400s were reclaimed from the RAF by the USAAF and served in combat in the Solomon Islands. This example is serving with the "Cactus Air Force", on Henderson Field, Guadalcanal during August 1942.

A P-40B of the American Volunteer Group in China—this early P-40 (Tomahawk IIA) carried two Browning AN/M2 .50 caliber machine guns in the nose, and a pair of Browning .30 caliber AN/M2 MGs in each wing. The first P-40s with the AVG in China were not equipped with bomb shackles.

A P-40F showing three Browning .50 caliber AN/M2 machine guns, with 235 rounds per gun, mounted in each wing. 79th Fighter Group, Italy 1944.

The .50 caliber wing guns of "Available Jones", a P-40F of the 86th Fighter Squadron of the 79th Fighter Group based in Italy during 1944. The P-40F featured a Packard-built Rolls-Royce Merlin engine.

P-40E of the 49th Fighter Group, on New Guinea during 1943.

The P-40B: note the twin Browning .30 caliber AN/M2 machine guns in the wings. The cyclic rate for the Browning .30 caliber aircraft gun was up to 1,500 rounds per minute (25 rounds per second).

P-40B of the 2nd Air Service Group wrecked in Iceland during October 1942. Note the detail on the long extension tube on the nose-mounted Browning .50 caliber guns.

Enemy ordnance: A P-47 Thunderbolt of the 318th Fighter Group shows off its wing-mounted .50 caliber MGs, along with a Japanese 132-pound bomb soon to be returned to its former owners. Saipan, July 1944.

Crew chief bore-sighting the Browning .50 caliber AN/M2 guns of a P-47 from the 19th Fighter Squadron. Saipan, July 1944.

The rugged and powerful P-47 Thunderbolt came to define the late war fighter-bomber. With eight .50 caliber MGs (425 rounds per gun) and up to 2,500 pounds of bombs the Thunderbolt was a dominating ground attack aircraft.

US .50 caliber firepower compared: the M45 quad .50 caliber MG mount used the Browning M2 HB (heavy barrel) infantry gun variant which had a much slower cyclic rate (575 rpm per gun) compared to the Thunderbolt's eight Browning AN/M2 (850 rpm per gun).

The aerodynamic cooling sleeves on the P-47's .50 caliber guns. A one-second burst from the Thunderbolt's battery of eight guns delivered about 115 rounds of .50 caliber armor-piercing (AP), armor-piercing incendiary (API), or armor-piercing incendiary tracer (APIT) rounds.

An experimental installation of a M2 20mm cannon under the wings of a P-47D, flown by Colonel Fred Gray of the 78th Fighter Group. The cannon added considerable drag and the additional firepower was not worth the handicap imposed on speed and maneuverability.

Profile view of Colonel Gray's under-wing 20mm M2 cannon, showing its muzzle brake and 60-round drum magazine. The aircraft was photographed at Duxford, England on October 24, 1944.

Some early versions of the P-51 Mustang Mk IA (using the Allison engine) were equipped with four M1 20mm cannons. The American M1 (a license-built version of the Hispano-Suiza) suffered from chronic jamming/misfires mostly due to an overly long chamber—a problem that was never corrected. Consequently, American Mustangs used the Browning .50 caliber AN/M2 machine gun.

A P-51A Mustang readied by civilian workers after its arrival in Glasgow, Scotland during October 1943. Note the installation of four .50 caliber MGs in the wings and the small bomb racks.

P-51B "Killer" (with a Malcolm Hood) of the 355th Fighter Squadron in England. The P-51B's wing gun installation was problematic - the guns canted on their sides and the ammunition belts feeding from an extreme curve from above. Firing during high-speed aerobatics often caused the belts to kink and jam.

P-51B showing its rather light armament of four .50 cal MGs. Note the odd angle of the weapon installation, which led to problems with jamming.

A field expedient remedy to the jamming problem of the P-51B's wing guns involved using an ammunition belt boosting motor taken from B-26 Marauder turrets.

The rare Douglas DGP-1 gun-pod mounted on a P-51B of the 368th Fighter Squadron during April 1945. The underwing pod contained two Browning AN/M2 .50 caliber MGs with 500 rounds per gun.

The light armament of the P-51B was not as much of a detriment when fighting more lightly constructed Japanese aircraft. This example is seen in China during late 1944.

The P-51A carried four .50 caliber MGs and up to 1000 pounds of bombs and rockets. This aircraft is part of the 311th Fighter-bomber Group, based in Burma in 1944.

Despite issues with the awkward axial tilt to its four .50 caliber MGs, the P-51B represented a significant breakthrough for 8th AF escort fighters. This P-51B is part of the 354th Fighter Squadron, in March 1944.

The P-51B offered good range (880 miles), high speed (440 mph), and four .50 caliber MGs with 350 rpg for the inboard guns and 280 rpg for the outboard guns.

The light armament of the P-51B was not as much of a detriment when fighting more lightly constructed Japanese aircraft. This example is seen in China during late 1944.

The P-51D introduced longer range, great pilot visibility with a teardrop canopy, and a six-gun armament with no reduction in performance. This is "Pauline" of the 339th Fighter Group, seen in early 1945.

Lt. Elmer Pankratz of the 160th Tactical Recon Squadron poses in front of his F-6D (P-51D Mustang tactical recon aircraft mounting two K-24 cameras). The F-6D retained the normal six .50 caliber machine gun armament of the P-51D.

The Mustang had horsepower and six-gun firepower: A P-51D 350th Fighter Squadron, England 1944.

P-51D of Lt Colonel Ben Irvin, commander of the 382nd Fighter Squadron taxis in at "A-15" field (Maupertius, France) during July 1944. This was the first Mustang to land in Normandy.

P-51D load out: the Mustang's six .50 caliber MGs carried a total of 1,840 total rounds, 380 rounds for the inner pair, and 270 rounds for the outer two pairs. This aircraft of the 332nd Fighter Group also carries two 75-gallon drop tanks.

A Douglas A-20G bomber converted at a USAAF base in New Caledonia into a P-70A night-fighter. Note the black paint scheme, the glazed nose, SCR-540 airborne radar, and a six .50 caliber MG armament.

One of the sixty original P-70 night-fighters built, equipped with SCR-540 radar and a ventral gun tray for four 20mm M1 cannons. Ammunition capacity was 120 rounds per gun.

The P-61B night-fighter was armed with four 20mm AN/M2 cannons (200 rounds per gun) in the lower fuselage and four Browning .50 caliber AN/M2 MGs (560 rounds per gun) in a dorsal turret, driven by a General Electric gyroscopic fire control computer.

P-61B "The Spook" wrecked on landing on April 20, 1945 548th Night Fighter Squadron on Iwo Jima. Note the details on the four-gun General Electric turret. The turret could be used by either the radar operator or gunner, whose positions had aiming control and gyroscopic collimator sights.

The shape of things to come: six new Browning .50 caliber AN/M3 MGs in the nose of the Lockheed P-80 Shooting Star (YP-80A) jet fighter. The AN/M3 was the fast-firing (1,500 rounds per minute) development of the Browning .50 caliber aircraft MG. The YP-80A was tested with the 1st Fighter Group, in Italy, April 1945.

A for Attack

MACHINE GUNS AND CANNONS FOR GROUND ATTACK

Six .50 caliber MGs of the Douglas A-20G “La France Libre” of the 9th Air Force, the first A-20 to complete 100 missions. France 1944.

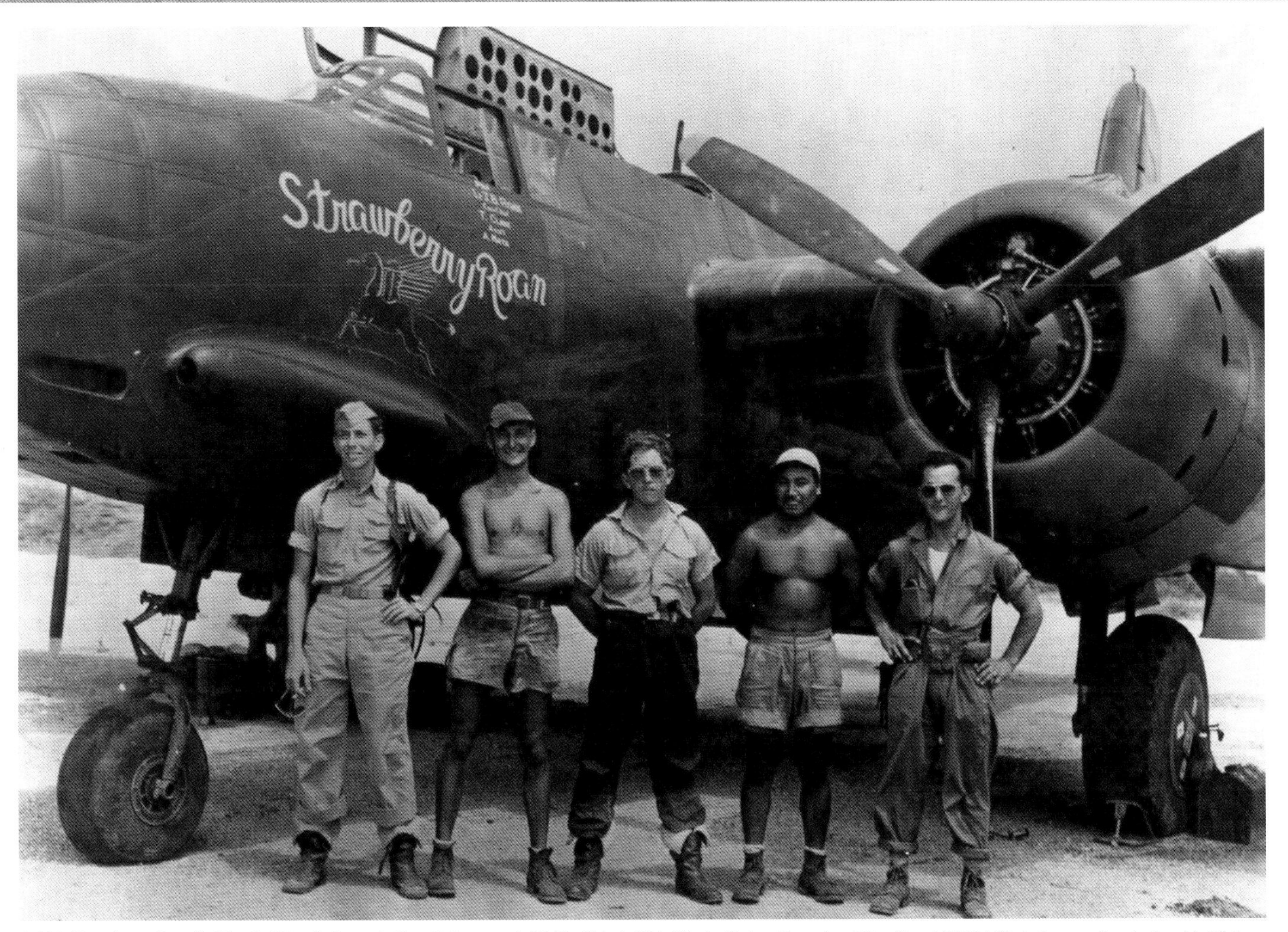

A-20A "Strawberry Roan" of the 3rd Bomb Group in New Guinea, early 1943. This A-20 is fitted with four Browning .50 caliber AN/M2 MGs in its nose (two in the side blisters and two in the lower faired nose).

A death's head gunship: "Eloise", an A-20G of the 312th Bomb Group shows off her six-gun nose (6x .50 caliber MGs). New Guinea 1944.

Servicing the Browning .50 caliber AN/M2 MGs of an A-20G of the 312th Bomb Group in New Guinea, 1944.

Details of the A-20A blister mounted .50 caliber Browning MG. North Africa, 1943

Factory-fresh gunship: A-20G with a six-gun nose.

Bound for Russia: An A-20C prepped for delivery to the USSR. Two .50 caliber MGs were mounted in blisters in the lower side of the glazed nose.

"Tutu", a field-modified A-20 gunship of the 47th Bomb Group with six .50 caliber MGs in its painted-over nose. Solomon Islands, 1943.

Soviet airmen prepare to ferry A-20Gs (fitted with four 20mm AN/M2 cannons) from Ladd Field, Alaska on to bases in Siberia in the USSR. Summer 1944.

The first group of 250 A-20Gs were equipped with the four 20mm cannon nose. Many of these were sent to the Soviets via lend-lease.

The nose of the A-20G, a bomber with built-in gunship armament of six .50 caliber MGs for strafing.

The nose of the A-20J lead ship for A-20 formation level-bombing missions. The A-20J retained two .50 caliber MGs in the lower nose.

The A-20G featured six .50 caliber MGs in the nose, a pair of .50 caliber MGs in the tail turret, and a single flexible .50 cal MG mounted behind the bomb bay. Maximum bomb load was 4,000 pounds.

The A-20 first debuted as a strafing gunship when field-modified by the 5th Air Force in the Solomon Islands campaign. Six forward-firing .50 caliber MGs in the nose became standard in the A-20G.

The first production run of A-20Gs were equipped with 20mm AN/M2 cannons in the nose. Most of these went to the USSR via lend-lease.

The A-26 Invader could carry up to 4000 pounds of bombs internally, and an additional 2000 pounds on underwing hardpoints. Six or eight .50 caliber MGs were carried firing forward in a "solid nose", and remotely controlled turrets (with twin .50 cal MGs) were in dorsal and ventral positions.

Douglas A-26B Invader of the 409th Bomb Group in Germany, April 1945. The A-26B carried either six or eight .50 caliber Browning MGs in its solid nose, and up to 6,000 pounds of bombs.

A-26B with an eight-gun nose. This aircraft of the 89th Bomb Squadron suffered a landing gear collapse at Kadena, Okinawa on August 11, 1945.

For additional firepower, the A-26 could carry underwing gun pods, each pod carrying a pair of .50 caliber MGs. These gun pods are similar to the later style cheek "blisters" mounted on B-25 gunships. This A-26B has 14 forward-firing .50 caliber MGs. France, spring 1945.

A-26B's of the 386th Bomb Group over Germany during early April 1945. All of these "invaders" carry four underwing .50 caliber machine gun pods, including the A-26J lead ship in foreground.

An A-36 in use as a low-level recon aircraft. Alaska, 1944. Note the details of the nose mounted .50 caliber MGs.

The A-36 was armed with two .50 caliber MGs in the nose, and four in the wings. Bomb load was normally two 500-pound bombs. This example served with the 527th Fighter Bomber Squadron, Italy, February 1944.

P-51A "Betty Jean" pushed into a revetment in the Anzio area, April 1944. This Mustang is one of the few P-51s armed with four 20mm M2 cannons.

Fitting 500-pound bombs to the wing racks of an A-36 dive bomber of the 527th Fighter Bomber Squadron, in Italy during 1944. The A-36 was noted for its overall reliability and accurate dive-bombing, but the ventral radiator was always vulnerable to ground fire.

MACHINE GUNS AND CANNONS IN OFFENSIVE AND DEFENSIVE ROLES

A hole in the roof. The radio operator's gun position in the B-17F "Hell's Angels" of the 303rd Bomb Group, June 1943

Men at work: B-17 waist gunners recap a busy mission over Germany amid a pile of spent .50 caliber casings. The gunners often sought to carry extra ammunition, but the added weight made for serious concerns.

Firing from an open window with no armor protection, this 8th Air Force B-17 waist gunner is seen during December 1943. His Browning .50 caliber MG is attached to a K-5 mount.

The later B-17G waist gun on the K-6 swivel gun mount, inside a three-pane plexiglass enclosure. This modification finally kept the waist gunners out of the freezing slip stream.

B-17 waist gun on a K-5 pedestal mount. The 200+ mph slip stream made a strong impact on the waist gunners.

Waist gunner aboard the "Memphis Belle". Confirming "kills" for air gunners was nearly impossible, with multiple planes and gunners firing at the same target.

Making movies: Browning .50 caliber AN/M2 equipped with a gunsight aiming point camera. These photos also show good details of the Bell Machine Gun Adapter (Model GM 43), a recoil damping device for .50 caliber MGs in "flexible" mounts. Without the damping effects of the adapter, the recoil forces of the .50 cal MG would make accurate shooting nearly impossible.

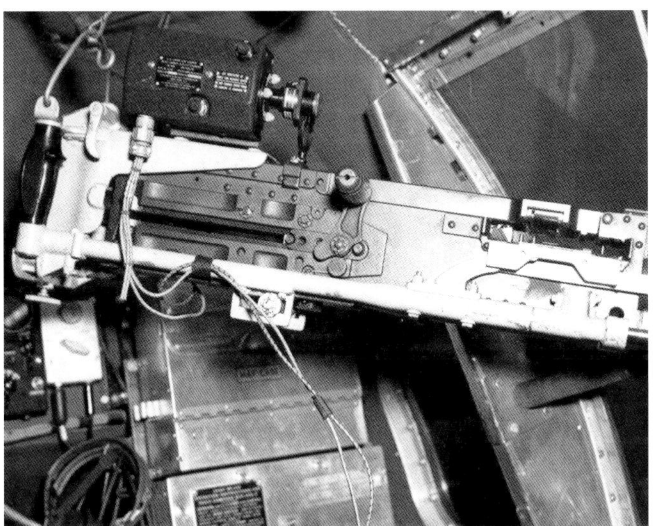

8th Air Force B-17 waist gunner wearing a flak apron in addition to electrically heated gloves and boots, late 1943.

8th Air Force B-17 waist gunner wearing an early style flak suit, November 1942.

The classic B-17 waist gunner, fighting from an open window in the freezing slip stream, manning a Browning .50 caliber MG and aiming with a simple ring and post sight.

The waist gunners of B-17F "Invasion II" of the 91st Bomb Group. Their guns are fed by disintegrating link belts attached to 250-round ammo boxes.

The crowded workspace of the B-17 waist gunner – each man had to be aware of the movements of the other.

B-17 waist gunner during July 1943. Note the metal 30-round ammunition box. The early, small ammo boxes did not allow for extended firing.

Medal of Honor winner Staff Sgt Maynard H. Smith (423rd Bomb Squadron) posing with a waist gun during July 1943. Smith was a ball turret gunner who won the MOH on his first combat mission.

The tight fit: Sperry ball turret of the B-17F "Hell's Angels" of the 303rd Bomb Group, in June 1943. Gunners needed to be small as the turret was tiny, and they did their work tucked into the fetal position.

At home in a bubble: Sgt Kenneth Long completed 50 missions as a ball turret gunner with the 8th Air Force during 1943. Gunners were strapped in as there was no room for a standard parachute.

In the belly: Ball turret of a B-17F of the 401st Bomb Squadron 1943. The receivers of the .50 caliber AN/M2 guns extended all the way to the back of the turret. Gun cocking was done by a cable.

B-17 ball turret: Normally, 500 rounds of ammunition was provided for each gun. For the ball turret gunner, clearing a jammed .50 caliber MG in combat was particularly difficult.

The gunners were responsible for the care of their weapons. This belly turret gunner of the 527th Bomb Squadron replaces the bolt on his Browning .50 caliber AN/M2 MG during 1943.

The "cheek" .50 caliber MG of a B-17F of the 324th Bomb Squadron, June 1943. Lt Leonard Cox wears a new style flak vest.

In response to increasing German fighter attacks from the head-on position, more and more .50 caliber MGs were added to the nose of the B-17F. The cheek guns had a particularly limited field of fire.

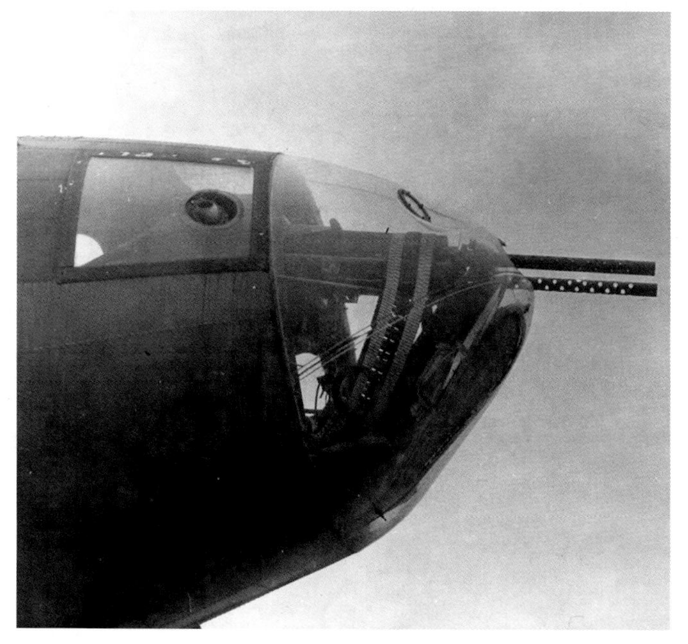

Some B-17Fs received a twin .50 caliber MG mount for their nose. This modification was useful, but also very bulky and difficult to maneuver in the tight space of the Fortresses' nose.

In the beginning: the earliest nose armament of the B-17 (in this case a YB-17) was a single .30 caliber AN/M2 machine gun. Langley Field, Virginia, May 1942.

An early .50 caliber AN/M2 machine gun in the waist blister of a YB-17. May, 1942.

The B-17G introduced the Bendix "chin turret", a twin .50 caliber MG position designed to protect against German head-on attacks. This turret was operated by remote control by the Bombardier. "Tiger Girl" of the 388th Bomb Group was lost over Bremen on November 26, 1943.

A .30 caliber AN/M2 MG in the nose of a B-17E. While the .30 caliber Browning was easily handled and particularly fast firing (1,500 rpm), its range was too short and striking power too light for effective bomber defense.

Pacific Fortress: "Yankee Doodle JR", a B-17E of the 11th Bomb Group, based at Espiritu Santo in late 1942. Note the .50 caliber MGs added to the nose, and the .30 caliber guns in the cheek positions.

The top turret: The "Sperry" top turret of the B-17F "Invasion 2nd" of the 401st Bomb Squadron.

Battle damage: Bomber gunners fought their war head-to-head against Axis interceptors.

After completing fifty missions over occupied Europe in late 1943, Sgt Manchester poses next to "Big Bertha", the Sperry top turret of his B-17F.

The Radio Operator's gun position was in the ceiling above the radio compartment. This example is seen on a B-17F of the 324th Bomb Squadron during May 1943.

The Bombardier of the B-17"Hell's Angels" (303rd Bomb Group) at his gun position during June 1943.

Radio operators in action: B-17F "Our Gang" of the 91st Bomb Group, June 1943.

Radio operator of a B-17F of the 91st Bomb Group.

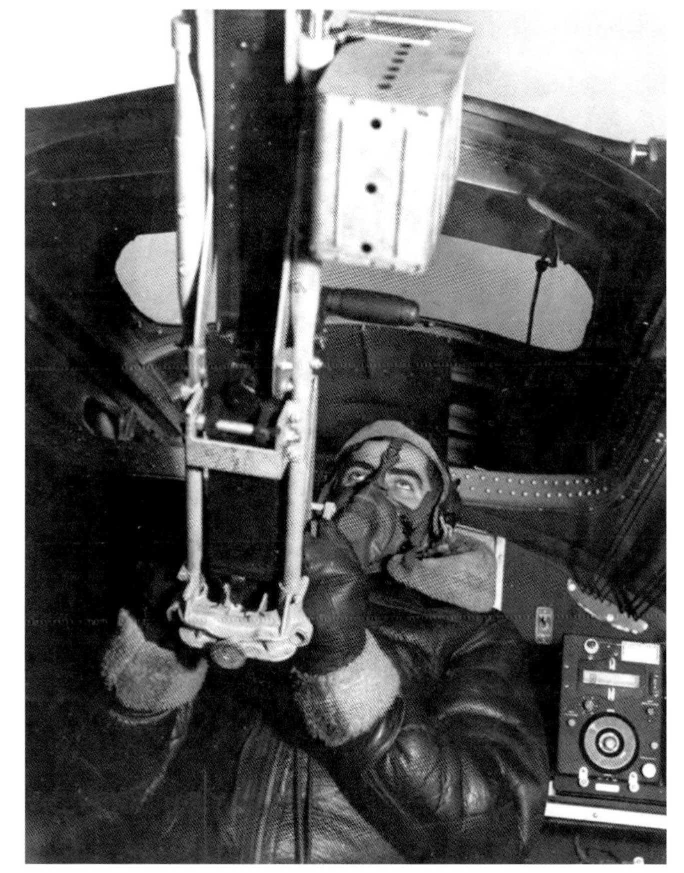
A good view of the B-17 radio operator's gun and its recoil-damping Bell Machine Gun Adapter.

The tail gun position of the "Memphis Belle". The guns were named "Pete" and "Repeat".

The tail guns of the B-17F "Hell's Angels" of the 303rd Bomb Group during June 1943.

A B-17's twin .50 caliber gun tail position split open by a hit from a German 20mm shell.

The .50 caliber AN/M2 guns of this B-17 tail position were equipped with flash hiders.

A tail gunner's odyssey: Staff Sgt James F. Jones fell out of the tail position without a parachute suffering only minor injuries, September 16, 1943. HIs B-17's tail struck a hill in bad weather and Jones fell out through the open escape hatch. The bomber then crashed into the subsequent hill and was wrecked.

The twin .50 caliber bite in the B-17's tail. Enemy fighters quickly learned to avoid intercepting a Flying Fortress formation from the rear.

The "Cheyenne" tail turret of the B-17G which offered the gunner a wider field of fire and featured a N-8 reflector sight for improved accuracy at range.

"Sherry's Hot Spot" shows off the details of the B-17F tail position. Note the simple ring and post gunsight.

The B-24 Liberator's electrically powered top turret was the Martin 250CE.

Top turret of a B-24 with the 755th Bomb Squadron, 8th Air Force, England August 1944.

This 8th Air Force B-24D has a twin .50 caliber MG package added to beef up its forward defences. It was damaged by a cable dropped by a German fighter over Emden during December 1943.

B-24H with the Emerson A-15 nose turret 450th Bomb Group January 1944 Italy 15th AF

B-24 waist gunners. The Liberator's waist position offered more room than the B-17, but the B-24 waist gunners still fought the bitter cold of the slipstream through the open window.

The Emerson A-15 nose turret of a B-24. With the 445th Bomb Group, based in England during April 1944.

B-24 of the 755th Bomb Squadron with the Emerson A-15 nose turret. The author's mother helped build these turrets.

B-24J with Consolidated A-6 rear turret. With the 755th Bomb Squadron, England, August 1944.

B-24L tail gunner during a raid on Wake Island, April 1944.

Pacific Liberator: In an effort to save weight, some B-24Ls were built with a simple, open twin-.50 caliber tail gun position. Note the flash hiders on the muzzles of the .50 caliber MGs.

Although not as celebrated as the Flying Fortress, the Liberator was still well-armed with 10 .50 Caliber AN/M2 machine guns in four turrets and two waist positions. This is a B-24J of the 9th Bomb Squadron, based in England during 1944.

Turning a bomber into a "strafer": This B-25C of the 490th Bomb Squadron (CBI) was equipped with the six .50 caliber AN/M2 machine guns. Note the details of the electrical firing system and the ammunition feed.

B-25C nose armament: one fixed and one flexible .50 caliber MG. "Missouri Waltz" is from the 446th Bomb Squadron in North Africa, July 1943.

A flak burst shattered this B-25's Bendix L-Type dorsal turret. The gunner luckily only received minor wounds. Note the armor plate that protected the gunner's head and back.

The sting in the tail: The .50 caliber rear gun of the B-25D. The position was extremely tight, with a very limited field of fire for the gunner.

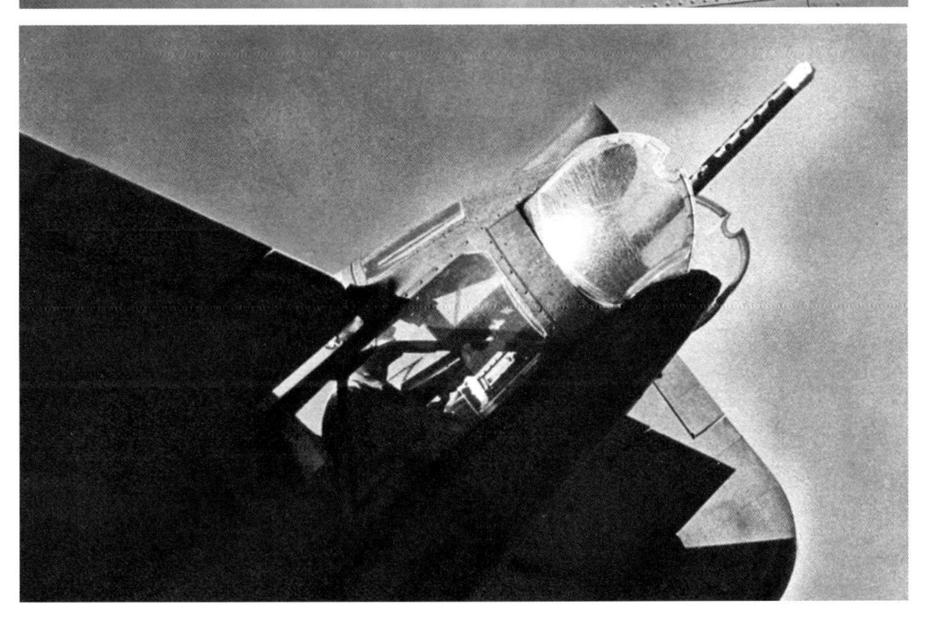

The eight-gun "strafer nose": A B-25J gunship prepared for a mission over the Japanese home islands, Ryukyu Retto, June 30, 1945. The extreme firepower of eight .50 caliber MGs was intensified by their tight grouping – this proved to be particularly dangerous to Japanese shipping.

Field modification: The B-25 strafers were the brainchild of Colonel Paul "Pappy" Gunn of the 5th Air Force. This is one of the early field-made gun pods attached to converted B-25 bombers. The critical Browning .50 caliber MGs were in short supply, and were often begged, borrowed, or stolen to equip the strafers. Note the modified, extended cooling jackets/blast deflectors.

The big gun gunship: Originally intended for anti-shipping operations, the B-25G featured a 75mm M4 cannon in its nose. Results with the slow-firing cannon were disappointing, and many cannons were replaced by a pair of .50 caliber MGs.

Cleaning the barrel of the 75mm M4 cannon of a B-25G 820th Bomb Squadron based on Tarawa during January 1944. The cannon was handicapped by a slow rate of fire (about four rounds fired in a normal strafing run) and the recoil impact on the B-25 was substantial. The cannon breech was located behind the pilot and was loaded by the navigator. When the gun was loaded, the navigator signaled the pilot who fired the cannon via a button on his controls.

The 75mm punch: The 75mm M4 cannon was a slightly modified version of the T8/M3 cannon which equipped many M4 Sherman tanks. This is a relatively rare B-25H-1–about 20 were made by Republic Aviation with the M4 cannon and just two .50 caliber MGs in the nose. China, March 1944.

The forward firing guns of a B-26B: four .50 caliber "package guns" mounted on the cheek positions, one fixed .50 caliber gun in the lower right, and the bombardier's flexible .50 caliber at the point of the nose.

B-26B "Hot Pistol" 552nd Bomb Squadron crash landed at Great Dunmow, August 1944. Note the ammunition feed and warming tubes for the bombardier's .50 caliber MG in the nose. The fixed nose gun (bottom left) has been deleted.

The Martin B-26B was well defended from the front. "Bad Penny" flew with the 554th Bomb Squadron, England, August 1943.

The .50 caliber package guns on the B-26 lower front fuselage, damaged by German 20mm fire over France, December 1943.

The top turret of a B-26 from the 386th Bomb Group, November 1943. The Martin 250CE turret was electrically powered in both azimuth and elevation.

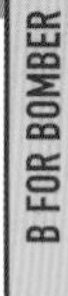

Flak damage: this plexiglass front panel of this B-26 top turret was smashed by a nearby flak burst.

The battle damage inflicted on this 8th Air Force B-26 shows off the details of its Bell M-6 tail turret. The B-26's .50 caliber tail guns had a generous 800 rounds apiece.

The Marauder's bite: The B-26G featured powerful armament for a medium bomber, with one .50 cal. MG in the nose, four in blisters on the fuselage cheeks, two in the dorsal turret, two in the tail turret, and two in the waist positions.

The four-gun top turret of "Ponderous Peg", a B-29 of the 871st Bomb Squadron based on Saipan, during November 1944.

The four-gun forward top turret of a B-29 with 52nd Bomb Squadron based on Guam in April 1945. The B-29's initially operated at high altitude and their guns were equipped with electric heaters (and were not oiled) to keep the weapons from freezing.

The B-29 featured the most advanced defensive gun system of any WWII bomber.

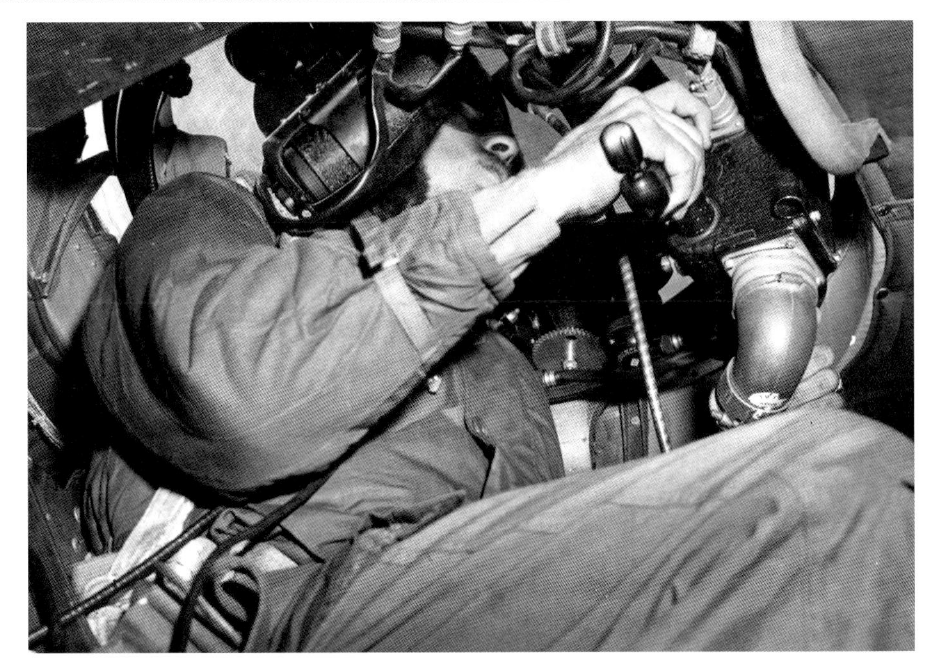

The B-29 used a General Electric Central Fire Control system with five interconnected firing stations. Each station had a GE analog computer that calculated the airspeed, necessary lead, gravity, and ambient temperature for the B-29 gunners.

Swabbing the barrels of a B-29's rear ventral turret. Saipan, 1944.

Servicing the forward lower turret B-29 of the 468th Bomb Group based in China (first arriving in April 1944)

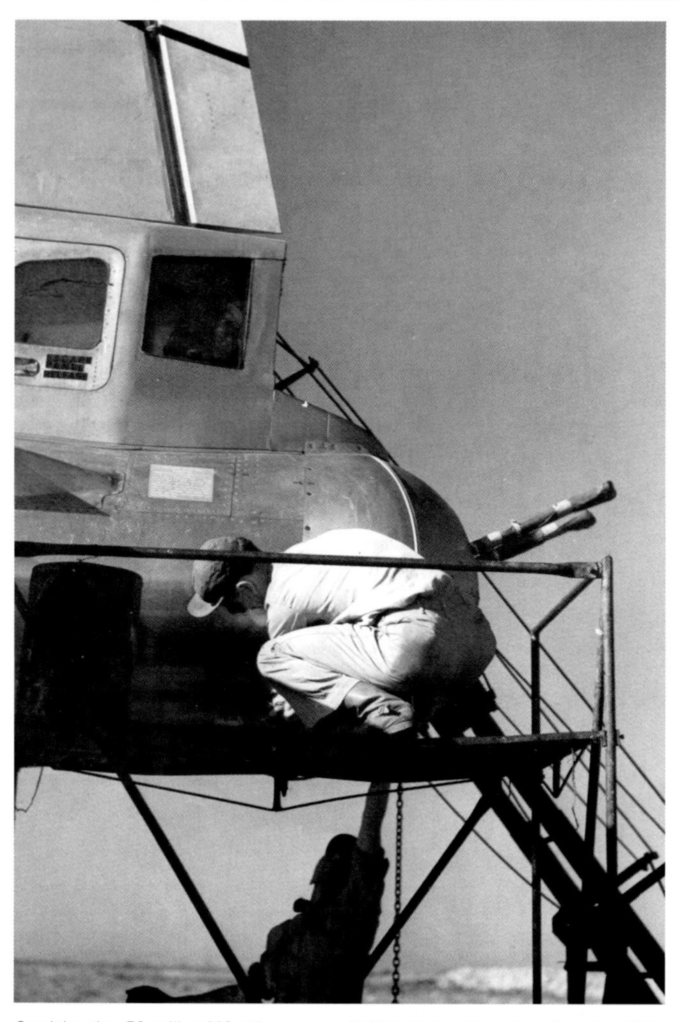

Servicing the .50 caliber MG tail guns on a B-29 in India after arriving from the USA.

The B-29 began its service life with a tail gun position that included a 20mm AN/M2 cannon. This example is seen with the 444th Bomb Group, based in China during late 1944.

The B-29's tail-mounted 20mm M2 cannon was provided with 120 rounds while the twin .50 caliber MGs had 1,200 rounds per gun. This B-29 is from the 468 Bomb Group, in India, summer 1944.

The 20mm M2 cannon was consistently dogged by a troublesome feed mechanism and frequent jamming. Ultimately the cannon was considered more trouble than it was worth and was removed to save weight.

The B-29's M2 tail cannon had a muzzle velocity of 2850 fps, a cyclic rate of 700 rounds per minute, and an effective range of 2,000 yards – more than enough to keep enemy fighters at bay. Unfortunately, the weapon never lived up to that potential.

Weapons maintenance

Feeding the Thunderbolt: the P-47 could carry a maximum of 425 rounds per gun.

The normal .50 caliber ammunition load for the P-47 was a combination of Armor Piecing (AP), Armor Piercing Incendiary (API), and Armor Piercing Incendiary Tracer (API-T).

Loading P-47 guns at Christchurch, England during 1944.

Armorers removing ammunition from a P-47 of the 318th Fighter Group after its flight from Saipan to Ryukyu Retto.

On the continent: Armorers attend to the eight .50 caliber MGs of a P-47 from the 366th Fighter Group at St. Pierre Dumont (A-1 airfield) in late June 1944.

Armorers synchronizing the .50 caliber guns of a P-47D.

Full service on Saipan: A P-47D of the 19th Fighter Squadron, gets the full treatment. June 25, 1944.

Armorers of the newly-arrived 19th Fighter Squadron bore-sighting the P-47s .50 caliber guns.

Swabbing barrels: Chinese troops help armorers of the 74th Fighter Squadron clean the six .50 caliber MGs at Kunming, China during February 1943.

Armorers load the P-40 of Colonel Robert Scott, commander of the 23rd Fighter Group in China. January 4, 1943.

Six-gun justice: loading the six Browning AN/M2 machine guns of a 11th Fighter Squadron P-40 based in the Aleutian Islands, September 1942. The P-40E carried 235 rounds per gun.

Armorers cleaning the Browning .50 caliber AN/M2 machine guns of a P-40F of the 79th Fighter Group, North Africa, March 1943.

Loading the four .50 caliber wing guns of an A-36 dive bomber during the North African campaign. Note the dive brake extending up behind the armorers.

Armorers service an A-36 after her 100th mission over Italy, late 1943. Note the .50 caliber machine gun in the lower nose.

The P-51D carried a total of 1880 rounds of .50 caliber ammunition: 400 rounds for the inner pair of guns, and 270 rounds for each of the outer two pairs.

Fusing MK4 5-inch HVAR rockets on a P-51D of the 78th Fighter Squadron on Iwo Jima during May 1945.

Servicing the canted wing guns (axial tilt) of a P-51B of the 15th Air Force in Italy during May 1944.

Loading the Mustang's guns: note the vast difference in access to the guns and ammunition feed trays between the P-51D (upper image) and the P-51B (lower image).

Armorers prepare 1,260 rounds of .50 caliber destined for a P-51B of the 374th Fighter Squadron, June 1944.

Clean guns shoot straight: An armorer swabbing the barrels of a P-51D.

Cleaning the barrels of the .50 caliber guns of a P-51B of the 15th Air Force, in Italy, May 1944.

The staggered guns of a P-51B of the 336th Fighter Squadron. This "canted" (axial tilt) arrangement gave some trouble with jamming during combat maneuvers. These issues were corrected with the P-51D.

Concentrated firepower: A P-38J of the 428th Fighter Squadron in England, September 1944.

The P-38's nose-mounted guns had an odd drawback. Cold air passed directly through the blast tubes and passed into the cockpit to chill the pilot who sat separated from the warming effect of the twin engines.

The squadron armament officer checks the 20mm ammunition for "Babe", a P-38G of the 48th Fighter Squadron August 1943. The P-38's 20mm AN/M2 cannon carried 150 rounds.

Preparing a P-38 of the 94th Fighter Squadron (based on Corsica) for Operation Strangle, the 15th and 12th Air Forces' aggressive air strikes on German supply lines in Italy during the spring of 1944

The P-38 Lightning was an armorer's dream as its centralized weapons bay was easy to access and service. In the air, the concentrated firepower meant that there was no "convergence point" – the weapons fired in a straight line ahead of the pilot.

NO STEP

A detailed view of the weapons bay of a P-38 of the 94th Fighter Squadron, with four .50 caliber AN/M2 MGs (500 rounds per gun) and one 20mm AN/M2 cannon (150 rounds). Corsica, spring 1944.

The Black Widow's bite: Armorers servicing the four Browning .50 caliber AN/M2 MGs (560 rpg) of the P-61's General Electric dorsal turret.

The Black Widow's bite II: servicing the P-61's weapons bay that housed four 20mm AN/M2 cannons (200 rpg). For the most part the M2 cannon performed well aboard the P-61.

PILOT

Lt. Haberman of the 6th Night Fighter Squadron shows off the first kill marking painted on his P-61 Black Widow. Saipan, July 1, 1944.

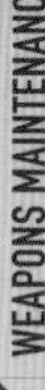

Tedious: hand-operated linking machine for .50 caliber MG rounds.

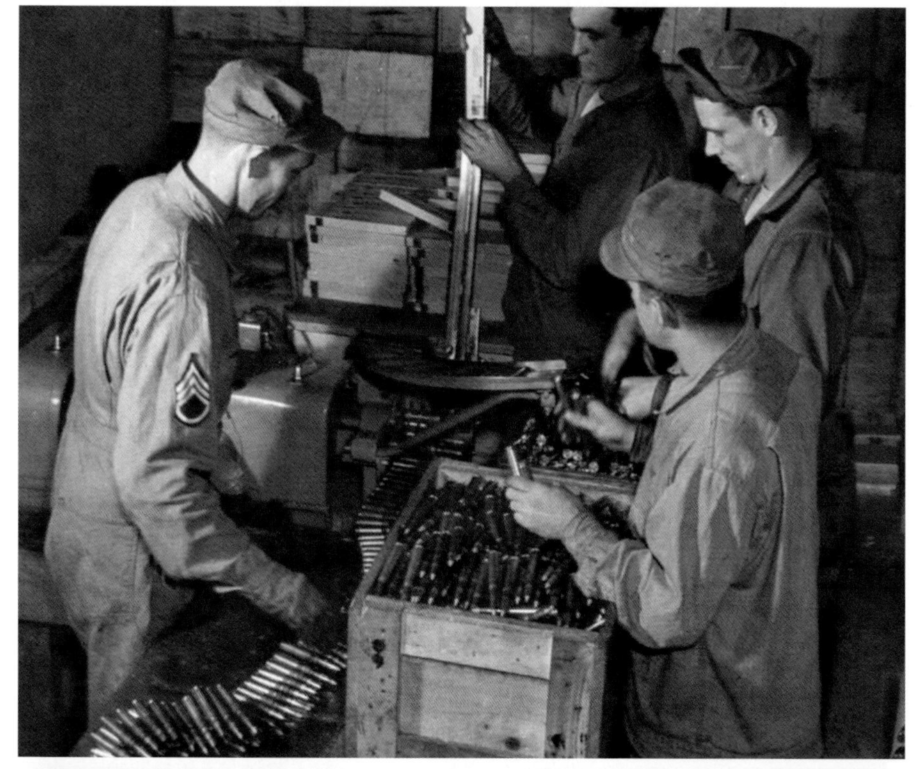

Linking tens of thousands of rounds of .50 caliber ammunition was a massive job that required manpower and a powerful linking machine. 8th Air Force ordnance depot, May 1944.

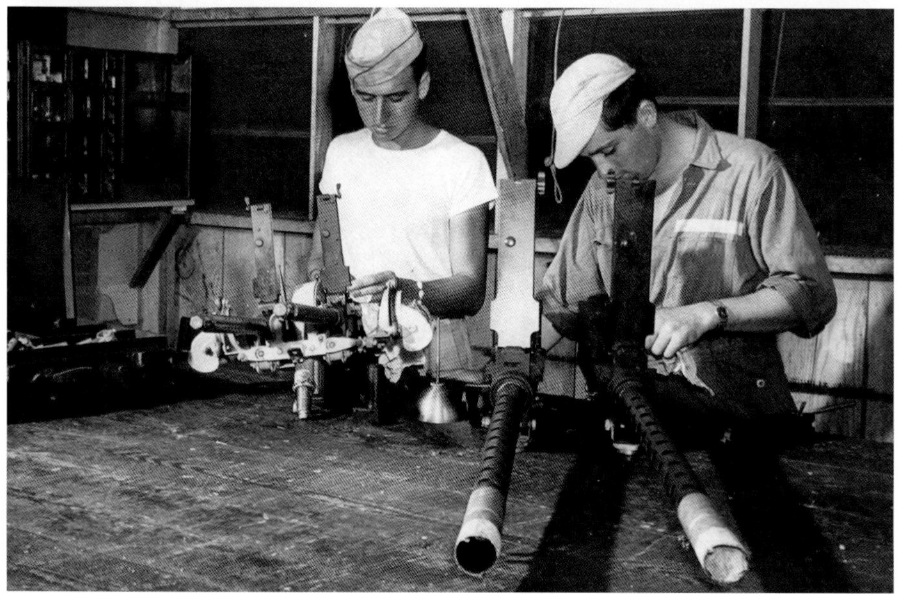

The Browning AN/M2 machine guns compared: the .30 caliber AN/M2 (twin) on the left, and the .50 caliber AN/M2 on the right.

With thousands of .50 caliber AN/M2 machine guns in service, and millions of rounds fired in action, the big Browning MGs proved to be the dominant aerial weapon of World War II. In that light, the USAAF armorers were the unsung heroes of the war to bring down the Axis.

Servicing the two .50 caliber guns of the rear turret of an A-20G. Philippines, late 1944.

An A-20 crew from the 646th Bomb Group, based in France during late 1944. The gunner displays his "flexible" (mounted in the rear belly, behind the bomb bay) .50 caliber AN/M2 MG with the Bell recoil damping device.

Cleaning the Browning machine guns of a B-17E based at Henderson Field, Guadalcanal, during November 1942. The .50 caliber AN/M2 is at left, while the .30 caliber AN/M2 is on the right.

Guns for the gunship: cleaning and oiling a Browning .50 caliber AN/M2 belonging to a B-25 gunship based on Tarawa during early 1944. Guns used in warmer climates and particularly at lower altitude were oiled, while guns used at high altitudes were not oiled to prevent freezing/jamming issues.

Gun simulators circa 1943: Airmen of the 401st Bomb Group in gunnery training with wooden mock-up MGs using gun camera footage.

Gunner trainee using a Browning .50 caliber AN/M2 on a K-6 mount with a Bell Machine Gun Adapter – recoil damping device. With the 401st Bomb Group, October 1944.

Gunnery training with live ammunition. 8th Air Force Bomber Command base, November 1943. The .50 cal MG is equipped with a Gun Sight Aiming Point camera.

Young guns: a gunner trainee gets the feel of the big Browning .50 caliber AN/M2 and its ring and bead sight.

A gunner trainee gets the feel of a Consolidated tail turret.

Learning to shoot on the move with your head on a swivel: a truck-mounted gun turret trainer in the Panama Canal Zone.

The guns of an ace: Armorers load the P-47 of Colonel Francis "Gabby" Gabreski of the 56th Fighter Group, the USAAF's leading ace in the ETO with 28 victories.

Desert sand gets into everything, particularly gun barrels and actions. Armorers carefully clean the .50 caliber AN/M2 guns of a 57th Fighter Group P-40. North Africa, 1943.

Armorers with a load of 20mm cannon shells for "Dangerous Dan", a P-61A of the 425th Night Fighter Squadron. The P-61's four 20mm AN/M2 cannons carried 200 rounds per gun. France, October 1944.

Loading the twin .30 caliber AN/M2 wing guns of a P-39D Airacobra based in Panama. Ammo load for the P-39's .30 caliber weapons was 1000 rounds per gun.

Swabbing the barrel of the 75mm M4 cannon-armed B-25G gunship, based in Panama.

Men of the 1st Brazilian Fighter Squadron cleaning the guns of their P-47 Thunderbolt in Italy, October 1944. Note the worn thermal sleeves on the .50 caliber MGs.

Rockets and guns: P-47D of the 56th Fighter Group equipped with M10 triple-tube launchers for the 4.5-inch M8 rocket.

Mustang firepower: armorers carry the six Browning AN/M2 machine guns and about 1/6th the ammunition load for a P-51D.

Cleaning the .50 caliber AN/M2 gun on a B-17G of the 532nd Bomb Squadron. This gun is in a K-6 swivel mount in the later style enclosed waist gunner position.

The .30 cal in detail

The pre war Colt-Browning .30 caliber (flexible) MG40 aircraft machine gun. Photographed at Aberdeen Proving Ground in 1929.

The .30 Caliber AN/M2 saw most of its service during WWII as a rear defense gun, particularly in the US Navy Douglas SBD Dauntless dive bomber (A-24 Banshee in the USAAF). The twin guns fired a combined 3,000 rounds per minute.

Manufacturing .30 caliber AN/M2 machine guns at the Buffalo Arms factory, May 1942.

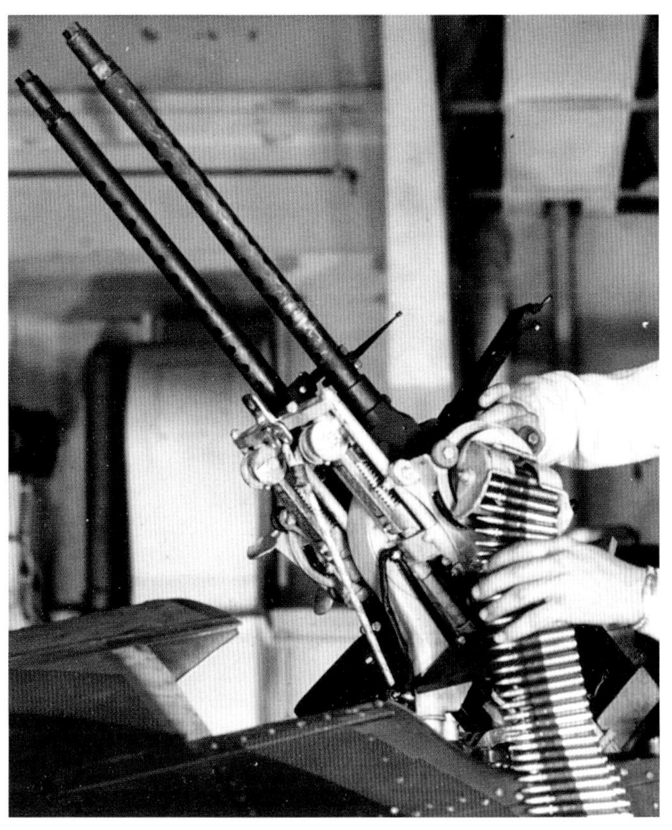

The twin sting in the tail: the rear guns of Navy SBD dive bombers found success against lightly constructed Japanese fighters in the early war period.

A .30 caliber AN/M2 in the nose of an early B-17. As a bomber defense gun, its rate of fire was excellent, but its range was too short.

An early twin .30 caliber aircraft gun setup with experimental drum magazines.

Good view of the .30 caliber AN/M2 gun mounted in the side blister of a Navy PBY Catalina.

The .30 caliber AN/M2 gun featured alternate-side feed. This example has a canvas bag to catch spent casings.

The ammunition box for the .30 caliber AN/M2 only held 100 rounds of belted ammo, barely enough for a few bursts from MG cycling at 1,500 rpm.

Air-dropped & launched ordnance

BOMBS CRADLES ROCKETS LAUNCH TUBES

The M10 triple rocket tube launcher for the M8 rocket was an impressive-looking weapon. However, it was inaccurate, and the range of the unguided rockets was short (maximum accurate range was 800 yards). This M10 launcher is fitted to a P-47D of the 19th Fighter Squadron on Saipan in the summer of 1944.

The powerful P-47 was the best choice to carry the M10 rocket launcher. This Thunderbolt is with the 65th Fighter Squadron, Italy.

An image of the common notion of the P-47 fighter bomber in Western Europe. While the Thunderbolts rarely destroyed German armor, they did savage Nazi motor transport across the ETO.

The M10 launcher was designed to be released after firing. When dropped, the attaching arms serve to direct the nose of the launcher downward as the air pressure pushes the tubes to the rear. Shown attached to a P-47 353rd Fighter Group, England, May 1944

The ability of the M8 rocket to hit an enemy tank is mostly myth. Even if it did hit, the M8 could only penetrate about an inch of armor plate. Shown attached to a P-47 313th Fighter Squadron, France, October 1944.

A somewhat rare installation of the M10 rocket tubes on a P-40. China, May 1944.

P-47 crewmen add the M10 rocket launcher to a 12th Air Force Thunderbolt, Italy, late summer 1944. The crew chief "owned" the aircraft, and if the pilot jettisoned the M10 launchers, he had to answer for their loss. Most squadrons had few replacements.

As the war progressed, use of the M10 rocket launchers became an issue of availability and the pilot's ability and comfort level with the weapon system. Attached here to a P-47D of the 65th Fighter Squadron, Italy 1944.

A Razorback P-47 of the 12th Air Force has its weapons aligned in Italy during 1944. Note the Cletrac M2 tractor lifting the Thunderbolt's tail. The M10 launchers were not popular with pilots or ground crews.

Sometimes called "rocket guns", each M10 triple-tube launcher weighed 98 pounds, while each M8 4.5-inch rocket weighed 40 pounds.

The M8 4.5-inch rocket. Its 5.1-pound warhead had approximately the same explosive energy as a 105mm HE shell. Penetration of the rocket warhead was poor; 1-inch of armor and about 1 foot of concrete.

P-47D "Jeanie" of the 64th Fighter Squadron, equipped with M10 rocket launchers and 250-pound bombs on the pylons.

A P-47N equipped with "zero-length" launch rails for the 5-inch High Velocity Aircraft Rocket rockets (the HVAR, sometimes called "Holy Moses"). The HVAR was more accurate than the M8 (by nature of its 1375 FPS velocity) and carried a much more powerful 45.5 pound warhead. Few HVARs were seen in the ETO, with the greatest use by USAAF aircraft in the closing days of the Pacific War.

M10 rocket-equipped P-40N of the 51st Fighter Group in China, May 1944.

A-36 in the CBI equipped with M10 rocket launchers. Note the .50 caliber machine guns in the lower nose. The heavy rocket tubes would greatly impact the Mustang's flight characteristics.

P-51A of the First Air Commando (CBI) equipped with M10 rocket launchers and a pair of 1,000-pound bombs. August 1944 - quite a heavy load for a Mustang.

M10 rocket tubes mounted on a P-51B of the 56th Fighter Squadron, China, July 1944.

Mustang rocketeer: P-51A of the First Air Commando, Assam, India August 1944. The M10 launcher was a poor weapon for the light Mustang.

The M10 rocket tubes were even tested on the tiny Bell P-39 Airacobra. The weight and drag of the rocket tubes were far too much for a small aircraft like the P-39.

The P-39 proved a capable ground attack aircraft in the Solomon Islands, carrying a maximum load of 500 pounds of bombs - but the M8 rockets and M10 launchers were never used operationally by P-39 units.

L-4 using 2.36-inch Bazooka rockets as improvised bombs, in support of the 158th Infantry Regiment, Philippines January 1945.

An L-4 (Piper Cub) of 9th Air Force Service command fitted with six 2.36-inch M1 "Bazooka" launchers. This aircraft was the mount of Major Charles "Bazooka Charlie" Carpenter, pilot of "Rosie the Rocketeer" near Nancy, France, September 20, 1944.

The triple M1 Bazooka launcher, mounted under each wing of Major Carpenter's L-4, used for attacks on the thin top armor of German AFVs. Carpenter was officially credited with six tanks destroyed by war's end.

Most of the Lightnings seen carrying the M10 rocket tubes served in the CBI. This rocket-armed P-38J is with the 459th Fighter Squadron, in India during 1944.

The M10 rocket tubes attached to the lower fuselage of a B-25.

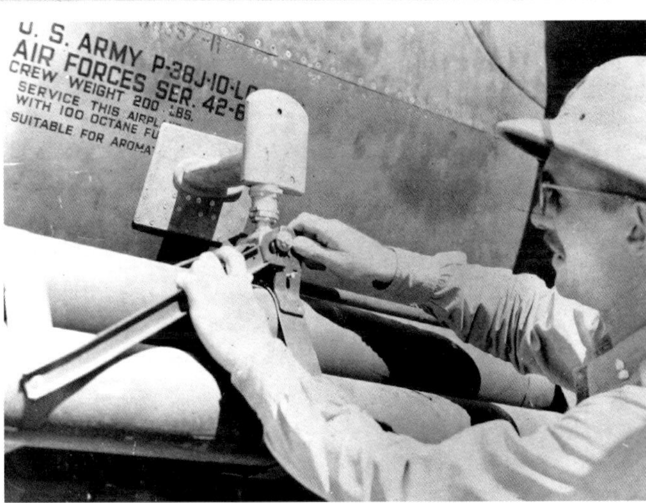

Attaching the M10 rocket tubes to a P-38 in the CBI.

The awkward M10 mounting on the P-38 Lightning. This would be dangerous to jettison and as the rearward flame jet of the rockets extends back 75 yards, the P-38s tail was likely to be scorched.

The small stabilizing fins on the 33-inch-long M8 rocket. Despite the launching tube, the M8 rocket was highly inaccurate.

A-20G 3rd Bomb Group, in New Guinea during July 1944, fitted with M10 triple-tube mounts under each wing.

Mechanics adding the M10 launchers (firing the M8 4.5" rocket) to the wings of the A-20. New Guinea, July 1944.

Detail view of the heavy, complex arrangement of the twin T10 launchers under the A-20 wing.

Twin T10 launchers beneath the wing of an A-20. 5th Air Force, New Guinea, July 1944.

Adding the impact-fuses (Rocket, Fuse M4) to M8 4.5" rockets. 12th Air Force, Italy 1944.

The T10 rocket launchers added considerable drag to the A-20, and the inaccurate rockets provided little in the way of useful firepower. Their use with the 5th Air Force became rare.

A 100-pound incendiary (M47A2) loaded aboard a P-47 Thunderbolt.

Loading an 8th Air Force B-24 with 20-pound AN-M41 fragmentation bombs.

Chemical Warfare: USAAF man wearing a protective suit (with respirator) carrying two smoke bombs. Aleutian Islands, April 1943.

Stacking up 100-pound incendiaries before an 8th AF mission.

A 500-pound incendiary cluster.

The 100-pound M47A2 incendiary bomb.

Above and below left: The M26A1 fragmentation bomb cluster consisted of twenty 20-pound AN-M41 fragmentation bombs.

Twenty-pound AN-M41 fragmentation bombs clustered around a AN-M88 220-pound fragmentation bomb on the belly rack of a P-47 of the 353rd Fighter Group, 1944.

M26A1 fragmentation bomb cluster on the wing rack of a P-47 of the 78th Fighter Group, July 1944.

A cluster of thirty 20-pound AN-M41 fragmentation bombs.

The 260-pound AN-M81 fragmentation bomb.

The AN-M40 "para-frag" hung up in the Philippines during July 1945. These weapons were particularly effective against Japanese airfields.

Clustered 20-pound AN-M41 fragmentation bombs.

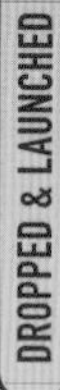

Loading a 500-pound general purpose bomb onto the wing rack of an A-26 Invader.

An M22 lift truck – capable of carrying up to 4,000 pounds of bombs.

500-pound bombs aboard an M5 bomb trailer, destined for a B-24D of the 328 Bomb Squadron April 1943. The M5 was rated to carry 4,850 pounds.

A AN-M65 1000-pound general purpose bomb loaded onto the external bomb rack of a B-17 of the 91st Bomb Group during September 1943.

B-17 of the 390th Bomb Group carrying a pair of AN-M65 1000-pound bombs on external racks September 29, 1943.

The 2000-pound GB-1 glide bomb had 12-foot wooden wings and was guided by a gyroscopic stabilization system – aimed by the bombardier. A few were used against Cologne, Germany with negligible results. Seen here with the 379th Bomb Group, June 1944.

M56 4000-pound general purpose bombs seen at the 8th Air Force Command Depot at Sharnbrook, England during July 1943.

8th Air Force B-17 loading 500-pound bombs from a M5 bomb trailer during April 1944.

8th Air Force bomb dump: A Chevrolet M6 bomb service truck works in the background.

Fusing 100-pound bombs in the bomb bay of an 8th Air Force B-24.

An M5 bomb trailer and a Chevy M6 bomb truck loading 500-pound general purpose bombs onto a 8th Air Force B-17G.

Loading a 500-pound general purpose bomb onto the wing rack of an A-20G of the 410th Bomb Squadron of the 9th Air Force, England, May 1944.

Personal messages: Loading a B-29 of the 500th Bomb Group with AN-M65 1,000-pound bombs. Saipan, 1944.

B-26 unloading AN-65 1000-pound bombs on German targets in France, 1944.

A B-26 of the 557th Bomb Squadron lets go a string of twenty-six 100-pound general purpose bombs over France, May 1944.

A 100-pound M-30 general purpose "spike bomb", used by the 10th Air Force in India to attack Japanese rail lines in Burma and India.

Loading a 250-pound bomb onto the wing rack of an A-20. Use of the wing racks significantly increased the A-20s bomb-carrying capacity.

Unusual ordnance: P-38 of the 459th Fighter Squadron loaded with a depth charge, at Chittagong, India during January 1945.

P-38 of the 82nd Fighter Group loaded with six 500-pound bombs (field modified with four additional hardpoints). Italy, 1944.

Loading a P-40K of the 64th Fighter Squadron with British 50-pound bombs. North Africa, 1943.

"You can't beat US": Inscribed 1000-pound bomb loaded aboard a P-40 of the 51st Fighter Group. Dinjan, India

P-40 of the 51st Fighter Group with a 1000-pound bomb India, June 1943.

P-40 of the 51st Fighter Group equipped with a 1000-pound bomb (see 148 B & C)

P-40 Warhawk fighter-bomber: 100-pound bombs beneath its wings and a 500-pound bomb on the centerline. The sturdy P-40s did yeoman work in ground attack throughout the MTO.

A P-40L is loaded with a 500-pound bomb on the centerline. Note that this aircraft has removed the outermost .50 caliber MG in its wings to save weight. Italy 1943.

Armorers load AN-M64 500-pound bombs aboard 79th Fighter Group P-40Fs. Capodichino, Italy, spring 1944.

P-47D fighter-bomber of the 81st Fighter Squadron loading a 500-pound bomb at Carentan, France (A-10 field) during July 1944.

A "Thunderbomber" of the 353rd Fighter Group loaded with a 500-pound bomb in December 1943. The 353rd pioneered dive-bombing with the big Republic P-47 fighter in the ETO.

This 12th Air Force P-47 carries the latest K-25 aerial camera built into the wing rack holding a 500-pound bomb. Italy, April 1945.

P-47 with a 500-pound bomb on its underwing rack. Saipan, 1944.

The workhorse: P-47 Thunderbolts effectively transitioned from an oversized fighter into a powerful fighter-bomber that bombed and strafed the Germans out of their "Fortress Europe".

Fusing a 500-pound bomb carried by a P-47 Thunderbolt of the 19th Fighter Squadron, Saipan, September 1944.

Heavy load for a fast horse: Loading a P-51 Mustang of the 374th Fighter Squadron (8th AF) with a 500-pound bomb—July 1945.

A French P-39 Airacrobra of the "Coastal Air Force" operating in the western Mediterranean. The P-39 could carry a 250-pound bomb on its centerline. This example is seen in Italy during the spring of 1944.

Christmas gifts ready for special delivery: A P-47 with a load of 500-pound bombs, addressed to Imperial Japanese Forces, from the Burma Banshees (80th Fighter Group of the 10th Air Force). December 24, 1944.

Operation Strangle: Loading 500-pound bombs aboard an A-36 dive bomber of the 527th Fighter-Bomber Squadron during the air offensive against German logistics in Italy, Spring 1944.

USAAF muscle: This A-36 dive bomber's ground crew loads 500-pound bombs by hand. North Africa, early 1943.

Men of the 333rd Fighter Squadron prepare "jell gas" (napalm) canisters for a P-47 Thunderbolt. Saipan, July 1944.

Armorers preparing napalm for a P-47 Thunderbolt of the 333rd Fighter Squadron on Saipan, late July 1944.

Arming the napalm firebomb (made from a drop-tank). With the 333rd Fighter Squadron on Saipan, July 1944.

Pumping "jellied gasoline" into a napalm canister before loading onto a B-17G, late March 1945.

Loading napalm canisters onto a B-17G in early April 1945.

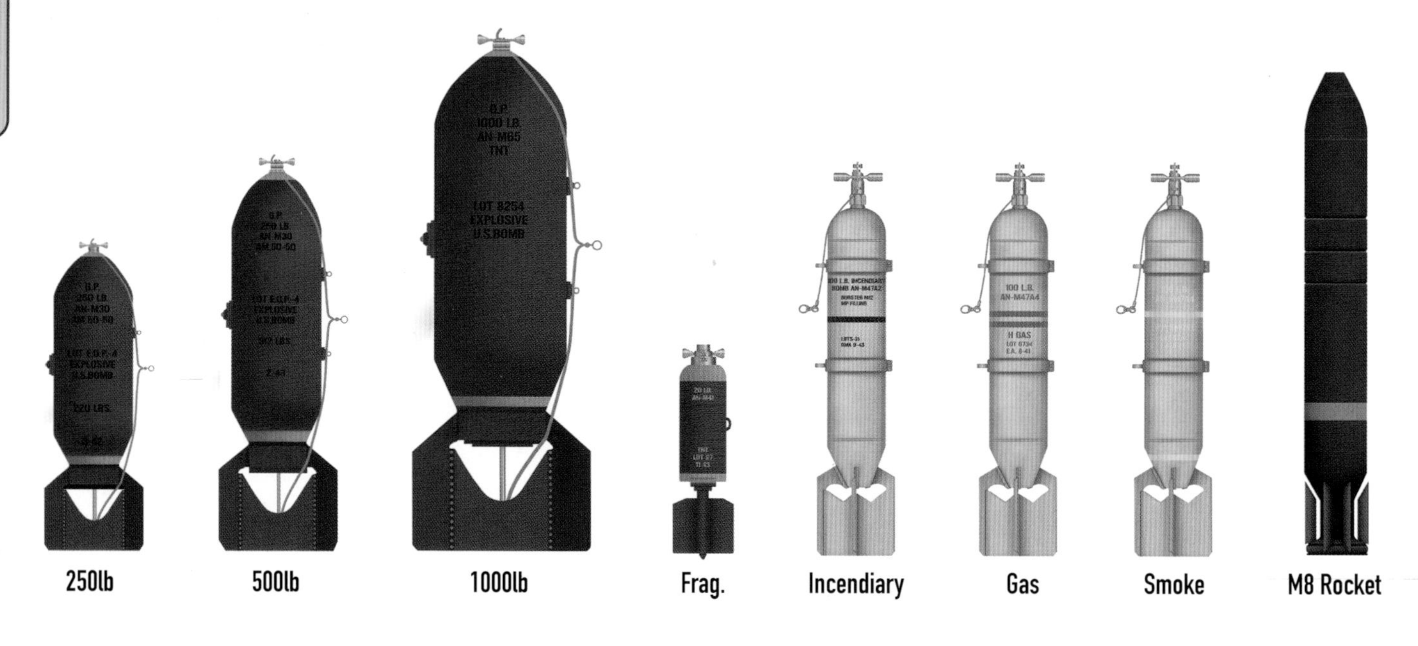

AERIAL BOMBS

CLASSIFICATION		WEIGHT	NOMEN-CLATURE	COLOR MARKINGS		HE WEIGHT	FUZES		SHACK-LES	MINIMUM SAFE BA	TARGETS AND REMARKS
				BODY	BANDS		NOSE	TAIL			
GENERAL PURPOSE		100	AN-M30	LUSTERLESS OLIVE DRAB	(1") YELLOW BAND AROUND NOSE AND TAIL	54	AN-M103 OR M118 OR M119	AN-M100A2 OR M112A1	B-7 OR B-10	1500	Railroad equipment, trackage, small buildings, ammunition dumps, planes on ground, hangars
		250	AN-M57			123				2000	Railroad equipment, trackage, RR terminals, ammunition dumps, destroyers, subs, transports
		500	AN-M64			262		AN-M101A2 OR M113A1		2500	Steel railroad bridges, subways, concrete docks, light cruisers
		1000	AN-M65			530		AN-M102A2 OR M114A1		3000	Reinforced concrete bridges, steel RR bridges, piers, approach spans, medium cruisers
		2000	AN-M66			1061			D-6	3000	Massive reinforced concrete and suspension bridges, heavy cruisers, battleships, dams
LIGHT CASE		4000	AN-M56			3245	AN-M103	AN-M102A2		3000	Raze areas equal to a city block or more
SEMI-ARMOR-PIERCING		500	AN-M58A1			145	STEEL PLUG	AN-M101A2	B-7 OR B-10		Armor plate, lightly armored vessels, reinforced concrete
		1000	AN-M59			303		AN-M102A2			
ARMOR-PIERCING		1000	AN-Mk33			144	NONE	AN-Mk228			Heavily armored naval vessels
		1600	AN-Mk1			215			B-10		
DEPTH		350	AN-Mk47			252	AN-Mk219 OR AN-M103	AN-Mk224 AN-Mk234 (LATERAL)	B-7 OR B-10		Submarines and surface craft
		650	AN-Mk29			464					
FRAG.	PARACHUTE	23	AN-M40			2.7	AN-M120A1	NONE	N-3	80	Personnel: If detonated at proper angle, almost 100% casualties over 120 ft. radius Tanks: Running gear, 60-90 ft.; light sank, direct hit Planes: Motor, 60 ft.; wings and tanks perforated, 200 ft.; structural damage, 3-4 ft. Telephone wires: 100 ft., same cut by side spray
	FIN	20	AN-M41			2.7	AN-M110A1			800	
	CLUSTER	500	M26				M111A2				
CHEMICAL MULTI-PURPOSE		100	M47A2	GRAY	*SEE BELOW	68	M108	BURSTER M4	B-7 OR B-10		Irritating physiological effect on personnel, neutralize areas, contaminate material. HS produces irritating physiological effect. WP produces screening smoke or incendiary effect
		115	M70			64	AN-M110A1	BURSTER M10			
INCENDIARY		4	AN-M50A1		1 PURPLE	1.8	NONE	STRIKER UNIT			Usually in 5 bomb clusters; includes 1 AN-M50XA1 1 150 gr. BP burster chargel
PRACTICE		100	M38A2	BLUE		2.6	NONE	MIA1			Training: 22 gage, light sheet metal body, filled with about 80 lbs. of dry sand. Actual weight, 98 lbs.
FLARES (PARACHUTE)		44	M24	GRAY	BLUE		NONE	FRICTION IGNITER		2500-3000	Target lightning, dropping rate, 11,6 ft./sec; burns 3-3,5 min; yellowish tint, 1 000 000 candle power
		53	AN-M26				M111A2			4000-25000	Target lightning, dropping rate, 11,6 ft./sec; burns 3-3,5 min; 800 000 candle power
		16	M8A1				NONE				Emergency landings; can be used for bombing. Burns 3 min, soft yellow, 400 000 candle power
TORPEDO		2100	Mk13-2			600	EXPLODER MECHANISM	NONE			Effective range, 6000 yds.; speed about 40 mph; has 93-98 hp steam and gas turbine engine

*BANDS: (NOSE, TAIL AND CENTER) 1 GREEN, NON-PERSISTENT; 2 GREEN, PERSISTENT; 1 PURPLE, INCENDIARY; 1 YELLOW, SMOKE; 1 RED, IRRITANT SMOKE (VOMITING GAS)